When I Take the Sacrament, I Remember Jesus

For Scott and my boys.
C. J. G.

To Cassidy and Madeline;
may you always remember.
S. J. C. T.

Text © 2012 C. J. Gudmundson
Illustrations © 2012 Shawna J.C. Tenney

Published by Covenant Communications, Inc.
American Fork, Utah

Copyright 2012 by Covenant Communications, Inc.
All rights reserved. No part of this book may be reproduced in any format or in any medium without the written permission of the publisher, Covenant Communications, Inc., P.O. Box 416, American Fork, UT 84003. This work is not an official publication of The Church of Jesus Christ of Latter-day Saints. The views expressed within this work are the sole responsibility of the author and do not necessarily reflect the position of The Church of Jesus Christ of Latter-day Saints, Covenant Communications, Inc., or any other entity.

Printed by Everbest Printing Co. Ltd, Nansha, China
First Printing: October 2012
108615

18 17 16 15 14 13 12   10 9 8 7 6 5 4 3 2 1

ISBN-13: 978-1-62108-020-6

When I Take the Sacrament, I Remember Jesus

Written by: C. J. Gudmundson

Illustrator: Shawna J.C. Tenney

When I take the sacrament,
I remember Jesus.

I remember Jesus was once a little child like me.

I remember Jesus showed me
the way to be happy.

I remember Jesus called prophets and apostles who teach me the things I should do.

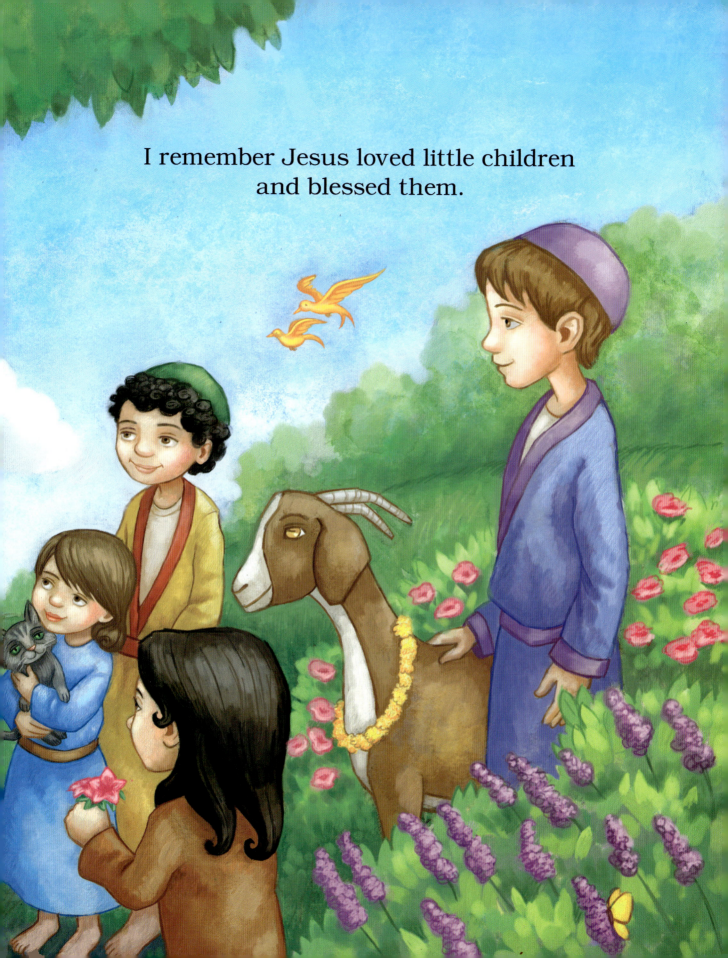

I remember Jesus said,
"Love one another."

I remember Jesus prayed to His Father,
and I can too.

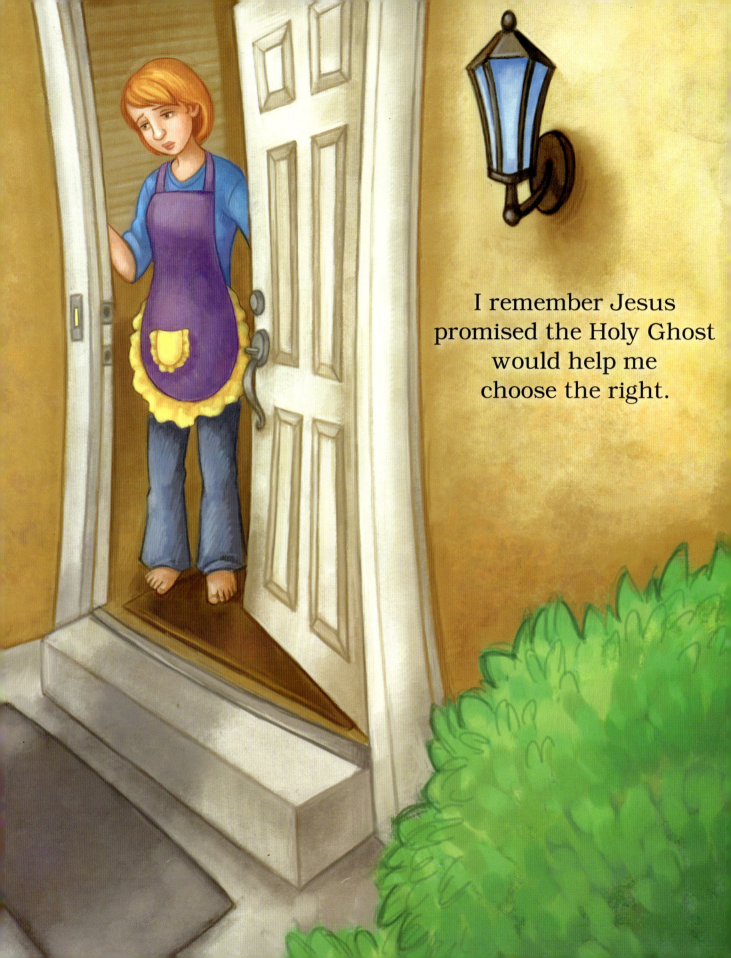

I remember Jesus promised the Holy Ghost would help me choose the right.

I remember Jesus established His Church. Today it is called The Church of Jesus Christ of Latter-day Saints.

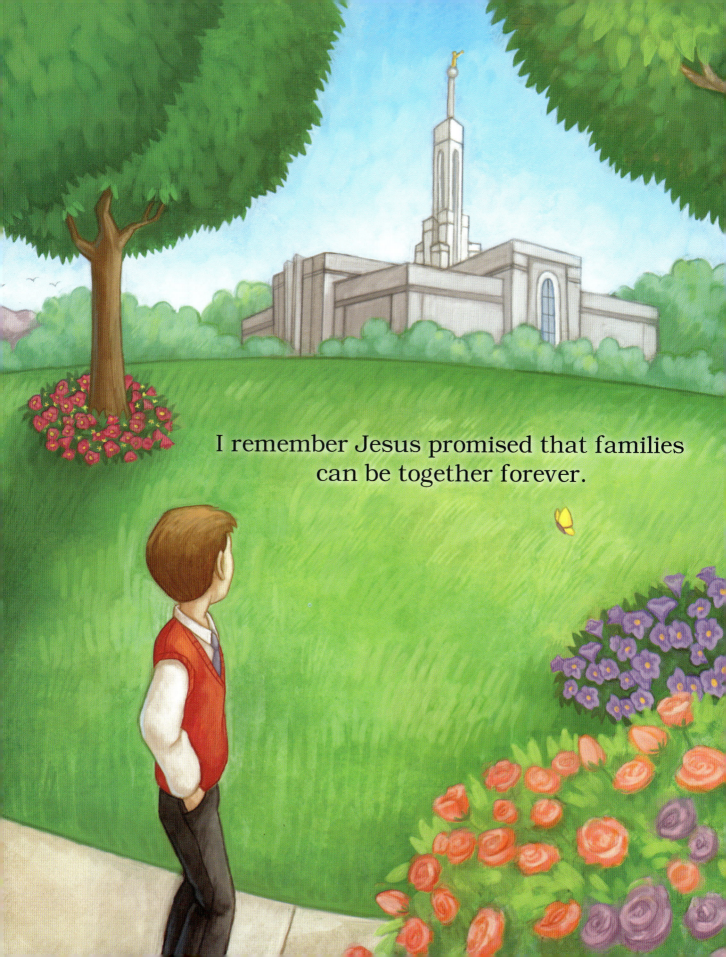

I remember Jesus wants me to be an example
and share His gospel with others.

I remember Jesus loves me.

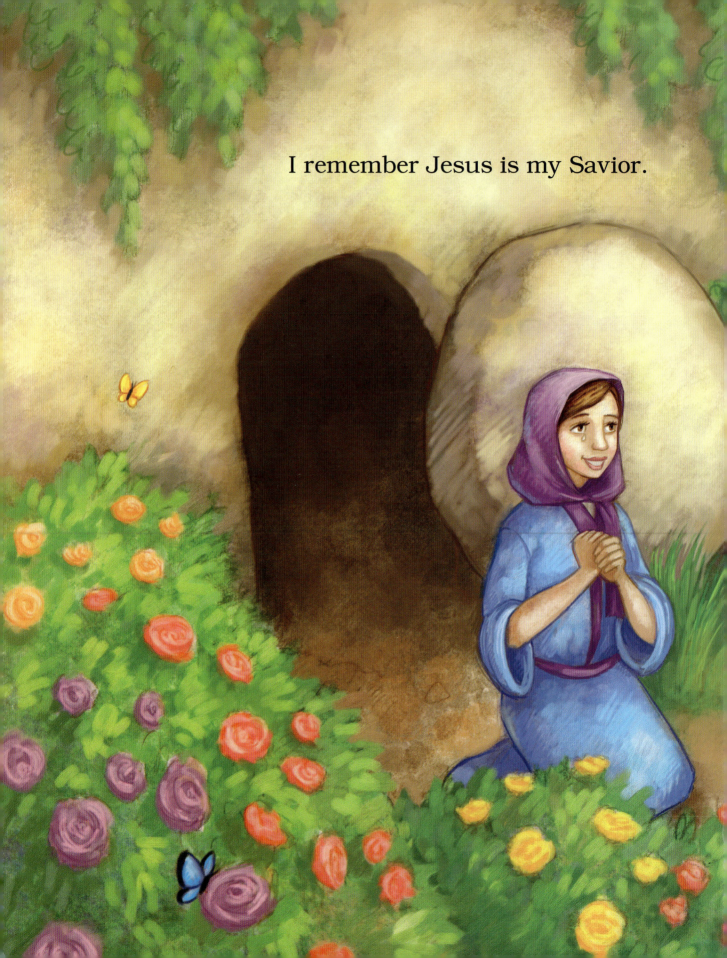

When I take the sacrament, I remember Jesus.